1 MONTH OF FREE READING

at

www.ForgottenBooks.com

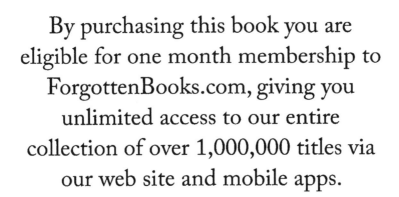

By purchasing this book you are eligible for one month membership to ForgottenBooks.com, giving you unlimited access to our entire collection of over 1,000,000 titles via our web site and mobile apps.

To claim your free month visit:
www.forgottenbooks.com/free1307576

ISBN 978-0-428-80474-9
PIBN 11307576

Historic, archived document

Do not assume content reflects current
scientific knowledge, policies, or practices.

W. I. A.—11.   Issued October 12, 1916.

United States Department of Agriculture,

BUREAU OF PLANT INDUSTRY

Western Irrigation Agriculture,

WASHINGTON, D. C.

LIBRARY RECEIVED OCT 14 1916 U. S. Department of Agriculture

THE WORK OF THE SCOTTSBLUFF RECLAMATION PROJECT EXPERIMENT FARM IN 1915.[1]

By FRITZ KNORR, *Farm Superintendent.*

INTRODUCTION.

The experiments reported in this circular deal chiefly with the problems of producing crops under irrigation in western Nebraska. Certain phases of the experimental work which was conducted on the farm in cooperation with other offices of the Bureau of Plant Industry and with the Agricultural Experiment Station of Nebraska are referred to only briefly. The details of these cooperative experiments will be published elsewhere. Many of the experiments in connection with the production of field crops under irrigation have been carried on for several years, and the present report deals with the results obtained in 1915, while summarizing the work of previous years.

During 1915 several experiments were started in connection with the work of establishing mixed-grass pastures on irrigated land to be used by dairy stock. The arrangement of the fields and the location of the experiments as conducted in 1915 are shown in figure 1.

CONDITIONS ON THE PROJECT.

WEATHER CONDITIONS.[2]

Although the weather conditions during the growing season of 1915 were in many respects adverse, the crop yields on the project were generally better than those of the previous year. The seasonal precipitation was the highest recorded since the farm was established. There were several severe storms during the season, notably a heavy snowstorm on May 18, which covered the ground to an average depth

---

[1] The Scottsbluff Experiment Farm is located on the North Platte Reclamation Project, 6 miles east of Mitchell and about 8 miles northwest of Scottsbluff, Nebr. The farm includes 160 acres of land, and the work is supported cooperatively by the U. S. Department of Agriculture and the Nebraska Agricultural Experiment Station. Operations on this farm were begun in 1909.

[2] The climatological observations at the farm are made in cooperation with the Office of Biophysical Investigations of the Bureau of Plant Industry, the necessary apparatus being furnished by that office.

of about 1 foot. This storm checked the growth of the first crop of
alfalfa and damaged it very materially, probably contributing to the
low average yield of that crop for the season. The spring season was
cool, cloudy, and backward. The last spring frost occurred on
June 12, nearly a month later than the normal date. The frost-free
period during the summer was the shortest during the five years
recorded. In addition to the late spring snowstorm referred to,
there were several severe hailstorms, which, though affecting relatively small areas, caused material damage within those areas. The

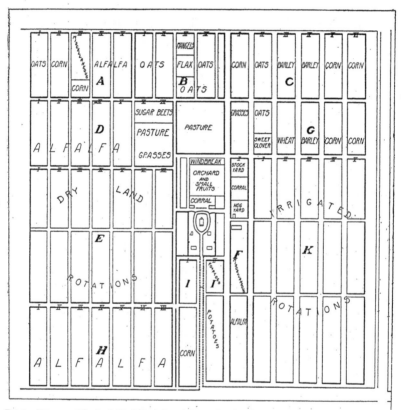

FIG. 1.—Diagram of the Scottsbluff Experiment Farm, showing the arrangement of the fields and location
of the experiments in 1915.

heaviest of these hailstorms occurred on August 6. It covered an
area of some 35 square miles near the center of the project, including
the experiment farm, where it was very severe. The crops of small
grains and the second crop of alfalfa, at that time nearly ready for
harvest, were so severely injured that in many cases they were en-
tirely lost. The corn crop was also severely damaged, while the
injury to potatoes, beets, and pasture lands was less severe.

The climatic data as recorded at the experiment farm are summarized in Table I.

Table I.—*Summary of climatological observations at the Scottsbluff Experiment Farm, 1911 to 1915, inclusive.*

PRECIPITATION (INCHES).

Year, etc.	Jan.	Feb.	Mar.	Apr.	May.	June.	July.	Aug.	Sept.	Oct.	Nov.	Dec.	Total.
1911	0.45	0.10	0	2.31	0.81	2.13	1,28	0.65	2.14	1.10	0.08	0.34	11.39
1912	.20	.60	.27	3.72	1.65	1.61	2.45	2.77	2.70	1.16	.37	0	18.51
1913	0	0	0	.13	3.70	1.71	1.30	4.33	1.18	.47	.11	.80	13.73
1914	0	.04	0	3.18	2.29	1.84	.39	.54	.24	.88	0	.36	9.76
1915	.15	.71	2.12	4.27	2.37	1.94	2.20	4.62	3.65	.90	.05	.60	23.58
Average	.16	.29	.68	2.72	2.17	1.85	1.52	2.58	1.98	.90	.12	.42	15.39

EVAPORATION (INCHES).

Year	Jan.	Feb.	Mar.	Apr.	May.	June.	July.	Aug.	Sept.	Oct.	Nov.	Dec.	Total.
1911					5.54	7.15	8.90	9.08	7.43	6.18			44.28
1912					4.24	7.14	6.64	6.67	6.32	4.16			35.17
1913					5.76	6.32	6.80	6.93	6.64	4.69			37.14
1914					4.60	6.42	7.17	8.42	7.91	5.77			40.40
1915					4.85	5.27	6.14	6.75	5.73	4.74			33.48
Average					5.00	6.46	7.13	7.57	6.81	5.11			38.09

DAILY WIND VELOCITY (MILES PER HOUR).

	Jan.	Feb.	Mar.	Apr.	May.	June.	July.	Aug.	Sept.	Oct.	Nov.	Dec.	
Mean:													
1911	6.1	6.4	7.8	8.4	8.8	6.0	5.2	5.4	5.4	5.9	6.8	4.9	
1912	5.4	5.7	6.7	8.6	8.1	5.4	4.0	4.2	5.0	5.0	4.3	6.4	
1913	7.0	4.7	5.8	7.2	7.7	6.1	4.1	3.3	3.8	5.1	3.6	4.5	
1914	5.6	5.6	7.3	7.4	6.2	5.2	4.3	4.7	4.8	4.0	3.7	5.1	
1915	5.3	5.1	5.4	6.4	6.1	6.5	4.4	3.1	4.0	3.9	5.6	4.2	
Maximum:													
1911	15.9	13.7	15.8	14.6	15.2	10.8	8.4	9.2	11.1	12.2	15.6	8.4	
1912	12.4	14.7	15.3	31.4	16.6	15.9	6.0	7.0	11.5	10.8	12.6	15.8	
1913	22.9	8.3	15.7	18.3	14.9	16.7	9.1	6.9	8.0	15.9	8.2	11.7	
1914	10.8	13.8	13.7	13.3	13.8	12.1	6.7	9.2	8.3	11.2	10.0	16.7	
1915	12.7	19.9	13.9	16.0	16.4	13.3	7.8	6.0	8.3	8.8	13.1	8.2	
Minimum:													
1911	1.7	2.1	3.0	3.6	4.8	3.0	3.1	2.6	2.9	2.5	1.9	1.2	
1912	1.6	1.4	2.7	3.2	2.9	1.6	2.0	2.6	2.4	2.0	1.1	1.3	
1913	1.9	1.0	1.5	2.5	3.7	.1	.4	.2	.1	.8	1.1	.8	
1914	2.1	1.3	1.9	2.9	2.9	2.1	1.3	2.5	1.7	1.9	.5	.3	
1915	.8	.4	.5	2.4	.1	2.7	1.7	.9	.9	1.5	1.3	1.3	

MONTHLY TEMPERATURE (°F.).

	Jan.	Feb.	Mar.	Apr.	May.	June.	July.	Aug.	Sept.	Oct.	Nov.	Dec.	
Mean:													
1911	29	27	42	45	46	70	69	68	64	43	32	24	
1912	20	24	21	45	55	63	69	67	52	47	39	27	
1913	22	15	31	46	57	64	69	72	56	56	39	14	
1914	31	22	37	45	57	66	74	69	62	43	40	21	
1915	22	30	27	52	51	60	67	66	58	50	38	31	
Maximum:													
1911	68	64	74	80	88	95	94	98	93	78	66	62	
1912	53	50	55	73	87	93	91	96	89	83	71	56	
1913	¹58	61	67	84	90	95	97	97	90	83	73	36	
1914	50	62	66	77	87	95	98	98	92	81	75	50	
1915	63	67	63	79	89	82	93	91	92	83	72	63	
Minimum:													
1911	−19	− 7	11	11	22	42	40	41	38	11	−12	−11	
1912	−21	−14	−15	25	30	39	47	44	22	12	3	1	
1913	−28	−18	−11	16	26	41	37	50	.24	12	13	− 9	
1914	8	−23	7	10	31	42	51	45	30	20	3	−15	
1915	−23	− 4	− 8	28	23	32	41	44	36	21	6	− 5	

KILLING FROSTS.

Year.	Last in spring.		First in autumn.		Length of frost-free period.
	Date.	Minimum temperature.	Date.	Minimum temperature.	
		° F.		° F.	
1911	May 26	28	Oct. 3	31	129
1912	May 13	30	Sept. 16	31	124
1913	May 2	26	Sept. 19	31	124
1914	May 7	32	Sept. 13	30	129
1915	June 12	32	Oct. 3	32	113

¹ 11 days.

CROP CONDITIONS.

Farm units to the number of 1,095, having a total irrigated area of 70,007 acres, were operated on the project in 1915. This shows an increase over the previous year of 151 farm units and 9,475 acres of land irrigated. The average farm value of crops per acre was estimated at $18.55, or $3.60 more than in 1914.

The acreage, yields, and farm values of crops produced in 1915 are shown in Table II, the figures being furnished by the United States Reclamation Service. The total cropped acreage shown in the table is less than the total irrigated acreage given in the preceding paragraph, because of the fact that 1,877 acres of land were sown to alfalfa without a nurse crop and, though listed as irrigated land, gave no crop. In addition to this, it is reported that 4,809 acres were seeded to alfalfa with a nurse crop, making a total of 6,686 acres of alfalfa seeded in 1915, or approximately 20 per cent of the normal alfalfa acreage of the project.

TABLE II.—*Acreage, yields, and farm values of crops produced on the North Platte Reclamation Project in 1915.*

Crop.	Area.	Yields.				Farm values.		
		Unit.	Total.	Average.	Maximum.	Per unit of yield.	Total.	Average per acre.
	Acres.							
Alfalfa hay	31,788	Ton	62,491	2.0	3.75	$5.00	$312,455	$9.83
Alfalfa seed	134	Bushel	121	.9	3.0	8.00	968	7.22
Corn	10,343	...do	209,626	20.0	80.0	.50	104,813	10.13
Sugar beets	7,872	Ton	97,753	12.5	23.0	5.50	537,641	68.30
Oats	7,112	Bushel	198,692	28.0	93.0	.40	79,477	11.18
Pasture	3,064						24,512	8.00
Barley	2,329	Bushel	87,037	37.0	104.0	.45	39,167	16.82
Wheat	1,878	...do	33,785	18.0	58.0	.90	30,406	16.19
Potatoes	1,395	...do	251,833	181.0	600.0	.40	100,733	72.21
Stock beets	276	Ton	4,498	16.3	40.0	3.00	13,494	48.88
Garden	219						4,071	18.58
Hay, native	181	Ton	137	.7	2.0	8.00	1,096	6.06
Rye	168	Bushel	1,551	9.0	21.0	.50	775	4.62
Millet hay	113	Ton	153	1.4	4.0	5.00	765	6.76
Millet seed	106	Bushel	1,444	13.6	30.0	1.00	1,444	13.62
Corn fodder	103	Ton	394	3.8	10.0	1.00	394	3.82
Beans	96	Bushel	987	10.3	40.0	3.90	3,849	40.09
Spelt	81	...do	1,729	21.0	75.0	.40	692	8.54
Cane for hay	63	Ton	130	.8	6.0	2.00	260	1.60
Onions	6	Bushel	990	165.0	250.0	1.00	990	165.00
Miscellaneous	803						5,614	6.99
Total	68,130						1,263,616	
Value per acre								18.55

The alfalfa acreage reported in 1915 is slightly less than that in 1914, notwithstanding a material increase in the total irrigated acreage of the project. From this it would appear that the present tendency among the farmers is to break up about one-fifth of the alfalfa land to use for other crops.

The most noticeable increases in crop acreage for 1915 are in corn, sugar beets, and wheat. The reasons for these increases are readily apparent. The farmers generally are beginning to realize the need of converting the heavy farm crops into live-stock products, in order to avoid the relatively high transportation costs of getting their products to market. Economical live-stock production involves the use of grain to supplement alfalfa, which is the most important crop on the project. Both corn and wheat are used as feed. The increase in the price of sugar beets for 1915 over that of 1914 stimulated the production of that crop.

LIVE STOCK.

There has been a sustained interest in the live-stock industries on the project. The present status of these industries is shown in Table III, which has been compiled from data collected by the United States Reclamation Service. These figures refer only to the live stock on the farms included in the Government project and do not cover the live stock on other farms in the upper North Platte Valley.

TABLE III.—*Live stock on the North Platte Reclamation Project in 1915.*

Item.	Inventory, Jan. 1.			Inventory, Dec. 31.			Increased total value.
	Number.	Value.	Total value.	Number.	Value.	Total value.	
Horses	4,618	$80.00	$369,440.00	5,508	$90.00	$495,720.00	}$146,480.00
Mules				202	100.00	20,200.00	
Cattle	3,190	45.00	143,550.00	6,941	50.00	347,050.00	203,500.00
Sheep	605	3.00	1,815.00	2,254	4.00	9,016.00	7,201.00
Hogs	22,143	8.00	177,144.00	24,928	8.00	199,424.00	22,280.00
Fowls	43,898	.40	17,559.20	46,971	.40	18,788.40	1,229.20
Bees, hives	476	3.00	1,428.00	630	3.00	1,890.00	462.00
Total			710,936.20			1,092,088.40	381,152.20

The most noticeable feature of Table III is the increase in the number of cattle during the year from 3,190 to 6,941. This does not include some 3,000 head that were brought on to the project during the fall of 1915 to be wintered or fattened for market. Of these cattle belonging on the farms there were 1,521 milch cows in the inventory of January 1, 1915, while on December 31, 1915, there were 2,218 milch cows. It is estimated that the returns from these milch cows during the year were about $23,000, while the sales of cattle other than milch cows amounted to $12,600.

There was also a marked increase in the number of sheep on the project farms, but the total number is not yet large. In addition to the sheep listed in the inventory, it is estimated that 85,000 head were brought in during the fall of 1915 to be fattened for market. The sales of sheep from project farms during the year, exclusive of those fattened for market during the previous winter, amounted to $1,600.

The increase in the number of hogs on the project farms was much less in 1915 than during the two previous years. There was a substantial increase, however, and the sales of hogs during the year reached a total of $230,000, or more than three times the sales of all other live stock, including dairy products.

The number of fowls increased slightly during the year. The receipts from poultry are given as $6,500 for the year and the receipts from bees as $500. The sales of horses during the year amounted to $29,800.

EXPERIMENTS WITH GRASS PASTURES.

The experiments with pasture grasses were begun in the spring of 1913, when 14 small plats were seeded with 11 different grasses and 3 clovers and 3 larger plats were seeded to 3 different mixtures of grasses and clovers. In the late summer of 1913 another plat, containing 1.7 acres, was also seeded to mixed grasses. These plats were pastured to a limited extent during 1914, but since the growth had not been very satisfactory it was not practicable to secure a quantitative statement of the results.

In 1915 these pastures were used intensively throughout the season by the seven head of dairy cows which were kept on the experiment farm. The pasture in field D (1.7 acres), which had been sown to mixed grasses without clover in the late summer of 1913, was used by four of the cows throughout the summer season of 108 days. It did not produce sufficient pasture for these four cows and was supplemented after July 12 by one-fourth acre of sweet clover. This made a total pastured area of 1.94 acres, but it was necessary to supplement this pasture still further with about 10 pounds of alfalfa hay per animal per day. The other pasture of 1.6 acres, which included two of the mixtures of grasses and clovers and also the small plats of the separate grasses, was grazed by three cows throughout the season of 108 days. This pasture was also insufficient for the cows, and they were fed about 10 pounds of hay per day in addition to the pasture.

From these preliminary experiments with pasture grasses it has not yet been possible to secure definite figures as to carrying capacity. It has been shown, however, that there are at least seven or eight of these grasses that thrive well under irrigation and a number of points essential to successful pasture management have been brought out. Among these points may be mentioned the need of frequent but light irrigations to secure the maximum growth. The use of alsike and white clover is to be recommended in preference to even a small quantity of alfalfa; the latter tends to cause bloat in cattle unless used very carefully. Of the grasses tried, tall oat-grass, smooth brome-grass, orchard grass, and meadow fescue seem to be the most promising. Bluegrass, western wheat-grass, perennial rye-grass, and timothy also do fairly well, though they appear to be less productive than those first mentioned. Italian rye-grass has shown a tendency to winterkill.

In order to provide for securing more definite information with reference to the behavior of these grasses when grown separately and in various mixtures, a new series of plats was started in field F in 1915. These plats were laid out 8 feet square, with 1-foot alleys between them, and were sown in duplicate on May 31 to the following grasses: Wheat-grass, smooth brome-grass, orchard grass, timothy, golden oat-grass, Italian rye-grass, perennial rye-grass, tall oat-grass, meadow fescue, sheep's fescue, tall fescue, redtop, bluegrass, red clover, white clover, alsike clover, sweet clover, and alfalfa. In addition to these duplicate plats of the separate grasses, a number of combinations of grass mixtures with clover were also sown, but these plats were not duplicated. The grasses were sown without a nurse crop, but the plats were covered with a light sprinkling of straw, to retain the moisture until after the seeds germinated. A good stand was secured on all plats, and the growth the first year was very satisfactory. The straw covering was removed on June 22, and on July 17 the growth on some of the plats was tall enough to be clipped with a lawn mower. Because of the admixture of chaff left from the mulch, the material clipped at this time was not included in the record of the season's growth. All the plats were clipped on August 4, again on August 21, and on September 4. After the September clipping, the Italian rye-grass, meadow fescue, tall oat-grass, alfalfa, and sweet clover made enough growth to be cut again, but it was desired to avoid the risk of winterkilling, so they were not cut. It was observed that several of the young grasses were injured by close cutting with the lawn mower; this was also true of the sweet clover and the alfalfa. The grasses in which such early injury was noted were wheat-grass, orchard grass, and timothy. The injury to the sweet clover was estimated as about 25 per cent of the plants.

The yields of forage from the three cuttings are given in Table IV, where both the green and dry weight are shown. These yields are also computed to the acre basis for greater convenience of comparison.

Table IV shows that some of the grass mixtures gave higher yields than the individual kinds. In order to afford more direct comparisons, a summary of the yields is brought together in Table V, which shows the average of the yields of the individual grasses which have been used in a mixture, together with the yield of the plat on which these kinds grew together.

It should be kept in mind that these yields are obtained from the first season's growth and should not be taken as indicating the later behavior of the plants, either separately or in the mixtures. The results are useful chiefly as showing quantitatively the growth that was produced during the first season.

TABLE IV.— *Yields of forage from plats of grasses, clover, and pasture mixtures, per plat and per acre, at the Scottsbluff Experiment Farm in 1915.*

Variety or mixture.	Number of times cut.¹	Plat yield. Green.	Plat yield. Air dry.	Acre yield. Green.	Acre yield. Dry.
		Lbs. Ozs.	*Lbs. Ozs.*	*Lbs.*	*Lbs.*
Wheat-grass	3	3 12.0	6.0	1,761	410.3
Smooth brome-grass	3	3 10.0	11.5	2,322	460.4
Orchard grass	4	6 2.0	1 1.5	3,924	700.7
Timothy	3	1 10.0	6.2	1,041	250.1
Golden oat-grass	4	3 2.0	14.5	2,002	580.1
Italian rye-grass	4	17	2 15.3	10,891	1,891.4
Perennial rye-grass	4	7 2.0	1 9.3	4,564	1,030.9
Tall oat-grass	4	7 5.0	1 12.0	4,684	1,120.9
Meadow fescue	4	6 2.0	1 8.0	3,924	790.6
Sheep's fescue	0	0	0	0	0
Tall fescue	4	8 7.0	1 6.7	5,405	910.8
Redtop	4	3 5.0	11.25	2,122	450.3
Bluegrass	3	1 2.0	4.0	727	160.1
Red clover	4	15 8.0	2 2.7	9,929	1,391.2
White clover	4	11 8.0	1 8.0	7,367	960.8
Sweet clover	4	8 8.0	1 5.5	5,445	880.7
Alsike clover	4	11 15.0	1 14.7	7,647	1,432.2
Alfalfa	4	11 8.0	2 1.5	7,367	1,341.2
Meadow fescue / Wheat-grass / Perennial rye-grass	4	6 12.5	1 3.5	4,344	780.7
Smooth brome-grass / Redtop	3	3 6.0	9.5	2,162	380.3
Bluegrass / Orchard grass / Italian rye-grass	4	18 9.5	2 15.0	11,911	1,881.7
Sheep's fescue / Redtop	3	3 0	8.0	1,921	320.3
Golden oat-grass / White clover	4	10 12.5	1 11.0	6.906	1,081.0
Sweet clover / Sheep's fescue	4	7 6.0	1 1.5	4,724	700.6
Meadow fescue / Orchard grass	4	7 10.5	1 5.0	4,904	840.7
Meadow fescue / White clover	4	9 13.5	1 8.0	6,305	960.9
Perennial rye-grass / Tall oat-grass	4	3 15.5	12.0	2,542	480.4
Bluegrass / White clover / Alsike clover	4	7 1.5	1 4.5	4,544	820.7
Orchard grass / Tall oat-grass	4	7 5.0	1 4.0	4,684	800.7

¹ Where four cuttings are shown, the yield of the first cutting, that of July 17, is not included in the weight given.

TABLE V.— *Yields of grasses from plats on which the crops were grown separately compared with the same kinds grown in mixtures at the Scottsbluff Experiment Farm in 1915.*

Grass mixtures.	Yield per acre, air-dry material (pounds). Mixture.	Yield per acre, air-dry material (pounds). Average of the same kinds grown separately.	Grass mixtures.	Yield per acre, air-dry material (pounds). Mixture.	Yield per acre, air-dry material (pounds). Average of the same kinds grown separately.
Meadow fescue, wheat-grass, perennial rye-grass	780.7	743.9	Sweet clover, sheep's fescue	700.6	430.3
Smooth brome-grass, redtop	380.3	455.3	Meadow fescue, orchard grass	840.7	745.6
Bluegrass, orchard grass, Italian rye-grass	1,881.0	917.4	Meadow fescue, white clover	960.9	875.7
Sheep's fescue, redtop	320.3	225.1	Perennial rye-grass, tall oat-grass	480.4	1,075.9
Golden oat-grass, white clover	1,081.0	770.4	Bluegrass, white and alsike clovers	820.7	851.0
			Orchard grass, tall oat-grass	800.7	910.8

ROTATION OF CROPS UNDER IRRIGATION.[1]

The irrigated rotation work, which was started in 1912, occupies 80 quarter-acre plats. Nine of these plats are used for the continuous production of each of the crops included in the rotations. There are eleven 2-year, three 3-year, four 4-year, and four 6-year rotations. The following are the crops used and the number of plats devoted to each: Alfalfa, 21 plats; beets, 14 plats; corn, 6 plats; flax, 2 plats; oats, 18 plats; potatoes, 13 plats; spring wheat, 5 plats; and winter wheat, 1 plat. One plat of corn and one of alfalfa are harvested by hogs, and the yields of these two are not included in Table VI.

P5775WI

FIG. 2.—Beloturka wheat before the hailstorm of August 6, Scottsbluff Experiment Farm. Photographed July 15, 1915.

The hailstorm of August 6, 1915, practically destroyed the spring wheat, oats, flax, and corn in these experiments, so that the yields have no significance. (Figs. 2 and 3.) The second crop of alfalfa was also badly injured, while the damage to the beets and potatoes was less serious. The winter wheat had been harvested before the storm.

Table VI shows that there was a rather wide range between the highest and lowest yields from plats devoted to the same crops. Each crop was seeded on the various plats at the same time, with the same kind of seed, and received the same cultural treatment after seeding, so that the differences in yield may be due in part to the sequence in the rotation and in part to the cultural treatment of the preceding crops.

---

[1] These experiments are supervised by Mr. James A. Holden, who prepared the report here presented.

Number of plats.	Crop.	Yield per acre.		
		Maximum.	Average.	Minimum.
20	Alfalfa...tons..	5.11	3.79	1.43
14	Beets...do....	16.35	12.98	8.23
13	Potatoes.......................................bushels..	231.50	153.10	65.10
1	Winter wheat...................................do....	37.00	27.00	27.00

Table VII brings out the most significant rotation effects in two important annual crops in the rotation experiment. The plats are arranged in the order of their yield, from the highest to the lowest.

P5776WI

FIG. 3.—Beloturka wheat after the hailstorm of August 6, Scottsbluff Experiment Farm. Photographed August 8, 1915.

Table VII shows that in every instance the highest yields were obtained from plats which either had grown alfalfa or had received one or more applications of manure. The manure was applied at the rate of 12 tons per acre.

The results of two years with beets following oats or potatoes which followed alfalfa are available. These results show an increase of 5.69 tons of beets per acre in favor of alfalfa land. An average of the results for four years shows that manure has increased the beet yield 4.24 tons per acre. The average results for three years show that manure has increased the total yield of potatoes by 64.9 bushels per acre and the percentage of marketable tubers by 14 per cent.

Hogging corn.—Four of the pigs used in the alfalfa-pasturing experiment were transferred to the corn plat on October 1, 1915. At this time the corn was practically all matured. Twenty-five days were required for the hogs to harvest the corn. During this time the hogs gained 216 pounds, or an average daily gain of 2.16 pounds per hog. The yield of the quarter-acre plat was estimated to be 13.10 bushels, or 52.41 bushels per acre. Valuing pork at 7 cents per pound, the hogs returned $15.12 per one-quarter acre, or $1.15 per bushel for the corn consumed. In other words, the hogs consumed 3.4 pounds of corn for each pound of gain. In the similar experiment conducted in 1914, hogs consumed 3.35 pounds of corn for each pound of gain.

EXPERIMENTS WITH ALFALFA.

Time of harvesting.—The test conducted in 1913 and 1914 to determine the effect of harvesting alfalfa at different stages of growth was again carried on in 1915 on 10 quarter-acre plats in field A–I. The plan of the test provides for harvesting the first plat in each crop at the time of the first appearance of the basal shoots and each succeeding plat at 5-day intervals thereafter. The test was conducted in duplicate on five pairs of plats, so that there was an interval of 20 days between the harvests of the first and last plats. In 1915 rains interfered seriously with the plan as to the dates of harvest. Because of this, in the second crop the first two pairs of plats were harvested on the same date and in the third crop the third and fourth pairs of plats were harvested on the same date. The dates of harvest and the yields obtained are given in Table VI, in which the yield reported is the average of two plats in each case.

TABLE VI.— *Yields of alfalfa (tons per acre) obtained in the time-of-cutting experiment on the Huntley Experiment Farm in 1915.*

First crop.		Second crop.		Third crop.		Three crops.
Date cut.	Yield.	Date cut.	Yield.	Date cut.	Yield.	
June 9.................................	2.21	July 27	1.67	Aug. 30	1.85	5.73
June 16.................................	2.30	...do......	1.78	Sept. 4	1.72	5.80
June 19.................................	2.81	Aug. 3	2.34	Sept. 14	2.05	7.10
June 24.................................	2.30	Aug. 6	1.97	...do......	2.05	6.32
June 29.................................	2.67	Aug. 11	1.92	Sept. 23	1.88	6.47

As shown in Table VI, there was no consistent increase in the yield of the first crop due to the delay in the time of harvest, nor did the yields of the second crop increase consistently as the growing period of the first crop was increased. But three crops were harvested in 1915, while in 1914 the first two pairs of plats produced four crops. The total yields indicate that a slightly higher yield results from delaying the harvest of the first crop, although the increase in the total yields was not consistent, the third pair of plats giving the highest yield.

Shrinkage determinations.—In order to learn whether the loss in weight of the alfalfa hay during the curing process is influenced by the time of cutting, determinations of the amount of shrinkage in alfalfa cut at different stages of growth were made in field A–I in connection with the time-of-cutting test. A 10-pound sample of green alfalfa was taken from each plat at the time of harvest. These samples were weighed and then thoroughly air dried in burlap bags hung in a dry shed. After drying was complete the samples were again weighed and the shrinkage was determined. The results of these determinations are given in Table VII, in which the loss of weight in drying is expressed as a percentage of the green weight in each instance.

TABLE VII.—*Determinations of shrinkage in alfalfa cut at different dates on the Huntley Experiment Farm in 1915.*

First crop.			Second crop.		Third crop.	
Date cut.		Loss in weight.	Date cut.	Loss in weight.	Date cut.	Loss in weight.
		Per cent.		*Per cent.*		*Per cent.*
June 9		76.7	July 27..	75.8	Aug. 30..	78.4
June 16		76.3	...do	75.1	Sept. 4..	77.8
June 19		75.9	Aug. 3...	75.7	Sept. 14 .	78.3
June 24		74.2	Aug. 6...	75.4	...do	75.9
June 29		74.1	Aug. 11..	75.1	Sept. 23 .	76.9
Average of 10 samples		75.4	....	75.4	....	77.4

The figures show that in the first crop there was a slight decrease in the amount of shrinkage as the growing period was increased. In the second crop there was but slight variation in the shrinkage. The average was 75.4 per cent in both the first and the second crop, while that of the third crop was 77.4 per cent. The average shrinkage for all three crops was 76.2 per cent, which was 0.1 per cent less than the corresponding average in 1914 and 0.5 per cent less than that obtained in 1913. The results of the shrinkage determinations made during the past three years seem to justify the conclusion that the shrinkage of alfalfa during the curing process on the Huntley project will average about 76 per cent of the green weight and that in but few individual cases will it differ greatly from this average.

IRRIGATED PASTURES.

Experiments with irrigated pastures were begun in 1911 and extended in 1913. The work at first was devoted to preliminary trials of a large number of pasture grasses to find which were the most promising. In 1914, and again in 1915, a carrying-capacity test was conducted on the plats which had produced the best growth in the preliminary trials, and in 1915 the experiments were extended so as to include several methods of getting pastures established. The results secured in these experiments in 1915 are briefly discussed below.

Establishing pastures.—A test of several methods of establishing pastures was started in 1915 in field B–V. In this test several pasture grasses and white clover were seeded separately, both with a nurse crop and without a nurse crop. The crops in this test and the rate of seeding per acre of each when planted, either with or without a nurse crop, were as follows: Awnless brome-grass (*Bromus inermis*), 14 pounds; orchard grass, 30 pounds; meadow fescue, 14 pounds; Kentucky bluegrass, 16 pounds; perennial rye-grass, 14 pounds; tall fescue, 14 pounds; and white clover, 2 pounds. The grasses were selected from those tried in previous years as being the most promising and best adapted to the region. The seeding was done on plats 6 feet wide and 170 feet long, containing 0.023 acre. The seed was planted with a grain drill on April 5.

On the same date these same grasses and white clover were seeded as a mixture on quarter-acre plats in the same field, both with and without a nurse crop. The constituents of the mixture and the rate of seeding per acre were as follows: Awnless brome-grass (*Bromus inermis*), 6 pounds; orchard grass, 5 pounds; meadow fescue, 4 pounds; Kentucky bluegrass, 5 pounds; perennial rye-grass, 6 pounds; tall fescue, 4 pounds; and white clover, 2 pounds; a total of 32 pounds per acre. The seed was planted through the grain hopper of an ordinary grain drill, as shallow as the drill could be made to run. Pringle Champlain wheat was used as a nurse crop and was seeded on the same date as the grasses at the rate of 1 bushel per acre. On half the plats seeded with a nurse crop, the nurse crop was cut for hay, and on the others it was allowed to mature.

The average yield of wheat on the plats seeded to separate grasses with a nurse crop was at the rate of 52.4 bushels per acre. On the plat seeded to the mixture with a nurse crop, the yield of wheat was at the rate of 47.3 bushels per acre. On the plats seeded to separate grasses with a nurse crop, the average yield of wheat hay was at the rate of 5.6 tons per acre. On the plat seeded to the mixture with a nurse crop, the wheat-hay yield was at the rate of 4.55 tons per acre. The plats seeded with a nurse crop were not irrigated until after the grain was harvested.

An excellent stand was secured with all the grasses seeded without a nurse crop except Kentucky bluegrass. These grasses made a very good growth during the season. A view of three of these grass plantings is shown in figure 4. On the plats from which the nurse crop was cut for hay, a good stand was secured of all the grasses with the exception of Kentucky bluegrass, and a fair growth was made after the hay crop was removed. The stand of grasses with a nurse crop that was harvested for grain was rather poor, much of the grass having died from drought before the grain was matured. Whether the grasses will recover sufficiently to make a good stand will not be known until next season.

Carrying capacity.—The test in which two cows were pastured during the season of 1914 on three quarter-acre plats of mixed grasses was continued during 1915. Two of these plats were seeded in 1913, one to a mixture of awnless brome-grass, orchard grass, perennial rye-grass, meadow fescue, tall fescue, Italian rye-grass, Kentucky bluegrass, and tall oat-grass, and the other to the same

FIG. 4.—Three of the grasses seeded without a nurse crop on the Huntley Experiment Farm. Awnless brome-grass on the left, orchard grass in the middle, and meadow fescue on the right. Photographed August 15, 1915, 132 days after planting.

mixture of grasses with the addition of alsike clover and white clover. The third plat in the test was seeded in 1911 to a mixture of awnless brome-grass, orchard grass, redtop, and timothy. In this test the two plats seeded in 1913 were placed in one inclosure and pastured alternately with the one plat seeded in 1911. The cows were on the part of the pasture containing the two plats for periods of from 10 days to two weeks and on the single plat for periods of five to seven days. Irrigation was applied whenever necessary to each part of the pasture as soon as the cows were removed. In 1915 each part was irrigated seven times. One-half of each part of the pasture was top-dressed with stable manure at the rate of 10 tons per acre in the fall of 1914. The beneficial effect of this treatment on the growth of the pasture was very apparent during the pasturing season.

corn to produce an equal quantity of grain. One season may be more favorable for one crop, and another for the other. In 1914 the average yield of barley on the project, as reported by the United States Reclamation Service, was 23.4 bushels per acre, which would be equal to a yield of about 21 bushels of corn per acre, while the average yield of corn, as reported for that year, was 15.5 bushels per acre. In 1915 the average yield of barley for the project, as given in Table II of this circular, was 37 bushels per acre, which is equivalent to 32 bushels of corn per acre, while the average yield of corn, as reported in Table II, is 20 bushels per acre. From these figures it would appear that barley is better than corn as a feed-producing crop on the North Platte project; but there are other factors to be considered, such as cost of production, effect in the rotation, and the seasonal labor requirements of the two crops in relation to the other crops grown.

The yields of the varieties grown in 1915 are shown in Table XI, together with the yields of the same varieties in 1914.

TABLE XI.— *Yields of barley varieties at the Scottsbluff Experiment Farm, 1914 and 1915.*

Variety.	Yield per acre.		
	1914	1915	
	Grain.	Grain.	Straw.
Two-rowed:	Bushels.	Bushels.	Pounds.
Hannchen	51.8	103.1	5,023
Moravian	91.6	102.2	5,499
Franconian	61.0	90.1	5,452
Svanhals	64.0	77.6	4,505
Hooded	40.0	71.0	5,099
Smyrna	65.1	53.2	4,195
Average	62.2	82.8	4,962
Six-rowed:			
Han.River	72.9	102.0	4,477
Barbary	72.2	101.0	4,594
Caucasian	29.1	100.5	5,370
Scotch	62.8	99.8	5,022
Coast (California Feed)	49.7	97.6	4,943
Mariout	53.9	93.6	4,829
Minnesota No. 105 (Manchuria)	37.0	88.5	4,418
Average	53.9	97.5	4,807
Average of both classes	58.0	90.1	4,884

OATS.

The oat varieties were sown in field C, Series II, on land that had been in alfalfa three years, 1911 to 1913, and in potatoes in 1914. There were 17 varieties in the test and the plats were duplicated. Two of the varieties, the Kherson and Iowa No. 103, were cut before the hailstorm of August 6. The other varieties were badly injured by that storm and had to be cut with a mower instead of a binder. The hail injury was not uniform throughout the series, partly because some of the varieties were more nearly ripe than others and suffered more and partly because the storm was apparently more severe over the south end of the series than over the north end. The yields of the varieties are given in Table XII, together with the yields for 1914 of the varieties that were grown in that year.

TABLE XII.— *Yields of oat varieties at the Scottsbluff Experiment Farm in 1914 and 1915.*

Variety.	Yield per acre.			Variety.	Yield per acre.		
	1914	1915			1914	1915	
	Grain.	Grain.	Straw.		Grain.	Grain.	Straw.
	Bushels.	*Bushels.*	*Pounds.*		*Bushels.*	*Bushels.*	*Pounds.*
Kherson	51.5	75.9	3,771	Dakota No. 4	66.4	41.1	6,333
Canadian	107.0	62.0	8,660	Danish	70.0	40.2	7,943
Iowa No. 103		56.7	4,439	Big Four	46.8	39.6	6,028
Wisconsin No. 1	42.8	52.8	7,238	White Russian		38.9	6,838
Newmarket	66.5	51.2	7,168	Swedish Select	73.7	38.9	5,616
White Plume	40.6	49.1	6,674	Garton No. 5		34.5	6,956
Golden Rain	66.4	43.6	8,001	Rustproof	48.1	34.1	6,027
National		43.1	7,590	Black Anthony	43.1	23.8	7,896
White Tartarian	67.1	42.1	6,901				

CORN.

Three lines of experimental work with corn were conducted during 1915, but the results in all cases were vitiated by the hailstorm in August. The first experiment was a test of 14 varieties, conducted in cooperation with the Office of Corn Investigations of the Bureau of Plant Industry. The second experiment was planned to determine the best time to plant corn, the plantings being made April 10, April 20, April 30, May 10, and June 1. Such results as were obtained from this experiment indicated that the planting of May 10 gave the largest yield and the greatest proportion of mature corn.

The third experiment was a comparison between planting corn with a lister and with an ordinary corn planter. The results did not show a significant difference in favor of either method.

STOCK BEETS.

There is a general interest among the farmers of the project in the possibility of using stock beets for forage. The range of varieties in common use is not extensive, and so far only five kinds have been tried. Of these, three varieties have been grown for three years, one variety for two years, and one for only one year. The variety test of 1915 was conducted in duplicate twentieth-acre plats in field B, Series III. The land had been in alfalfa in 1912, in potatoes in 1913, and in sugar beets in 1914. It was manured in the fall of 1914. In view of the fact that the tops as well as the roots of the stock beets have some forage value, the yields of both roots and tops were determined. The weight of the tops is for the air-dry condition. These yields for 1915 are given in Table XIII, together with the yields of roots for the varieties that were grown in 1913 and 1914.

TABLE XIII.— *Yields of stock beets, roots and tops, at the Scottsbluff Experiment Farm in 1915, together with the yields of roots for 1913 and 1914.*

	Yield per acre (tons).				
Variety.	1913	1914	1915		3-year average.
	Roots.	Roots.	Roots.	Tops.	Roots.
Half-Sugar beets	32.0	17.5	22.0	0.96	23.8
Yellow Globe mangels			21.6	.81	
Danish Sludstrup mangels		19.6	18.4	.57	
Giant Red mangels	36.5	17.8	18.2	1.00	24.1
Yellow Tankard mangels	38.1	14.4	14.5	.74	23.5

There is a preference among feeders for the Half-Sugar beets rather than the mangel-wurzels, but this may be due to the belief that they are richer in sugar and consequently of higher feeding value. No feeding results are available to determine this point. Any satisfactory basis for comparing the feeding value of stock beets and sugar beets is also lacking. Stock beets may be expected to yield from 30 to 50 per cent more than sugar beets, and they are also very much cheaper to harvest, but it is not known whether or not these advantages are offset by a lower feeding value.

POTATOES.

The experiments with potatoes in 1915 included a test of varieties,[1] a continuation of the test of different classes of tubers for seed, and a test of different cultural and irrigation methods. In addition, a number of new seedling varieties were propagated in 1915, to be included in the variety test of 1916.

VARIETY TEST.

Ten varieties of potatoes were tested in 1915, of which six were named varieties and four were seedlings. These four seedlings have been retained as the best from among 50 seedling lots received for trial in 1911. The test was conducted in triplicate rows in field I, Series II, on land that had been in small grain the two preceding years. The results of the test are shown in Table XIV.

Until 1915 variety No. 15411 has given good results; this year more than one-half of the yield was culls.

[1] Conducted in cooperation with the Office of Horticultural Investigations, Bureau of Plant Industry.

18

TABLE XIV.— *Yields of potato varieties at the Scottsbluff Experiment Farm in 1914 and 1915.*

Variety.	Yield per acre (bushels).				Variety.	Yield per acre (bushels).			
	1914		1915			1914		1915	
	Market-able.	Culls.	Market-able.	Culls.		Market-able.	Culls.	Market-able.	Culls.
No. 4452 [1]	223	66	227	56	Irish Cobbler	233	90	136	62
Pearl	192	48	221	61	Sophia × Keeper [1]			117	81
No. 8114 [1]	170	78	154	84	Early Ohio	142	48	96	63
Triumph	83	55	149	62	Albino	251	57	92	62
Eureka	259	66	146	47	No. 15411 [1]	192	40	79	98

[1] These are the four stocks that were retained from 50 seedlings received from the Office of Horticultural Investigations four years ago.

No disease was found among the potatoes during the year. The only damage done was by hail, and on three occasions, after heavy rains, a very large portion of the series was submerged in water. After the first hailstorm the water stood on the field for nearly two days.

IRRIGATION AND TILLAGE EXPERIMENTS.

Experiments with potatoes were conducted on duplicate plats in field I, Series II, on land that had been in alfalfa in 1913 and 1914, for the purpose of ascertaining (1) whether some variation of the usual methods of irrigating the crop influences either the total yield or the yield of marketable tubers, and (2) whether on the light soil of the experiment farm it pays to give special attention to deep ditching between the rows in preference to the ordinary methods of nearly flat cultivation. A belief is current among irrigation farmers that deep ditches should be maintained between potato rows, in order to wet the ground well below the plants. This method of cultivation involves the use of special attachments to the cultivators and is rather more troublesome and expensive than ordinary flat cultivation or slight ridging, and, furthermore, the high ridges expose a larger area of surface soil to the air and probably increase the loss of water by evaporation.

The present experiments included five different methods of irrigation, which are enumerated below:

Method A: Irrigation confined to alternate furrows, the same furrow being irrigated each time.

Method B: Irrigation in every furrow as often as is necessary to keep the plants growing well.

Method C: Irrigation in alternate furrows, the furrows which are left dry at one irrigation being irrigated the next time.

Method D: Irrigation given in every furrow, as in B, but delayed each time until the soil is dry and the plants begin to suffer for water.

Method E: Irrigation given in every furrow and more frequently than in method B, so that the plants always have an excess of water.

In one set of these irrigation experiments, as enumerated above, the cultivation was shallow and the ridges were kept low. In the other set, designated as A-1, B-1, etc., the cultivation was deep and the rows were ridged up at each cultivation. The results of this experiment for 1915 are given in Table XV.

TABLE XV.— *Yields of potatoes, resulting from different methods of irrigation and tillage at the Scottsbluff Experiment Farm in 1915.*

Method.	Yield per acre (bushels).			Per-centage of culls.	Method.	Yield per acre (bushels.)			Per-centage of culls.
	Mar-ket-able.	Culls.	Total.			Mar-ket-able.	Culls.	Total.	
Shallow:					Deep:				
A	102	51	153	50.0	A-1	96	47	143	49.0
B	132	49	181	37.8	B-1	123	47	170	38.2
C	122	47	169	38.5	C-1	89	35	124	39.3
D	90	55	145	61.1	D-1	110	45	155	40.9
E	115	54	169	47.0	E-1	96	61	157	63.5

This experiment has been carried on for four years, and the results are summarized in Table XVI, which gives the yield per acre of marketable tubers from each method each year and the average for all four years.

TABLE XVI.— *Yields of marketable potatoes resulting from different methods of irrigation and tillage at the Scottsbluff Experiment Farm, 1912 to 1915.*

Method.	Yields per acre (bushels).				4-year average.	Method.	Yields per acre (bushels).				4-year average.
	1912	1913	1914	1915			1912	1913	1914	1915	
Shallow:						Deep:					
A	193	177	164	102	158.7	A-1	181	134	145	96	139.0
B	186	155	223	132	174.0	B-1	183	126	202	123	158.6
C	208	195	181	122	176.2	C-1	191	176	168	89	155.9
D	195	179	173	90	159.3	D-1	179	143	182	110	153.4
E	200	172	218	115	176.3	E-1	169	178	263	96	176.6
Average	196	175	192	112	168.9	Average	180	151	192	102	156.7

Table XVI shows that there is very little difference in yield to be expected in a series of years as a result of the different methods of irrigation or ditching. It should be kept in mind that the soil on which these experiments were conducted is a light sandy loam into which the irrigation water penetrates rapidly and that similar results might not follow on heavy soils; also, that the results from the different frequencies of irrigation are interfered with materially by rain. This was particularly true in 1915, when the rainfall was much above normal.

SEED STOCK.

The experiments to determine the effect of planting different kinds of seed on the yield of potatoes have been carried on for three years; but only the 1914 and 1915 results are comparable, because the experiments in 1913 did not include all the classes used later. These classes are as follows:

(1) Field run; tubers picked up as they came in the field.

(2) Field selection; the seed taken from the best hills in the plat, selected at digging time.

(3) Bin selection; the best-looking tubers, selected from the bin at planting time.

(4) Culls; small tubers, selected from the bin at planting time.

(5) Immature seed; tubers obtained without special selection from a plat planted late in the season in order that the plants would not be mature at digging time. In other respects this class is comparable to the field-run seed.

(6) Whole tubers; selected from the bin at planting time, using tubers weighing 6 to 8 ounces each. These are comparable to the bin selection, except that the whole tuber is planted, while in the other cases the seed is cut to one or two eyes to the piece.

In these experiments the seed for planting is selected from a plat that was planted with the same class of seed the previous year. Two varieties were used, the Pearl and the Eureka. The results for 1914 and 1915 are shown in Table XVII.

TABLE XVII.— *Yields of potatoes in the seed-stock experiments at the Scottsbluff Experiment Farm in 1914 and 1915.*

	Yield per acre (bushels).						2-year average marketable (bushels).
Variety and class of seed.	1914		1915			Percentage of culls.	
	Total.	Marketable.	Total.	Marketable.	Culls.		
Pearl:							
Immature seed	207.6	130.5	327.4	243.7	84	25.5	187.1
Bin selection	154.3	101.1	251.6	158.3	93	37.1	129.7
Culls	183.3	127.2	199.1	128.3	71	35.5	127.7
Whole tubers	131.6	61.6	205.3	139.5	66	32.0	100.5
Field selection	200.5	128.3	123.2	68.8	54	55.8	98.5
Field run	178.6	85.5	127.0	66.6	60	52.4	76.0
Eureka:							
Immature seed	353.3	289.1	257.0	183.7	73	28.5	236.4
Whole tubers	367.0	288.3	241.6	175.1	65	27.1	231.7
Field selection	336.6	296.2	141.1	89.5	52	36.5	192.8
Culls	329.0	271.2	200.4	112.5	88	43.8	191.8
Bin selection	305.0	252.5	179.9	116.6	63	35.2	184.5
Field run	320.8	260.8	160.8	95.4	65	40.6	178.1

The results in 1915 were consistent for both varieties except in the case of the bin selection of Eurekas, which gave a low yield; and the yields for both years show the distinct superiority of immature seed for planting and the relatively lower yields to be expected from the use of field-run or even field-selected seed when the field selection is not done with particular care. The superiority of the immature seed is shown not only in the yield but during the growing period as well. (See fig. 4.)

CULTURAL METHODS WITH SUGAR BEETS.

DEPTH OF PLOWING.

In order to determine whether the depth of plowing influences the yield of sugar beets, an experiment has been conducted for the past four years in which this was the only variable factor in a series of plats. Each year the plats for beets have been plowed to the depth of 4, 8, 12, 16, and 20 inches, a subsoil plow being used behind the turning plow in the last three cases.

P5771WI

Fig. 4.—View of potato seed-stock experiment, Scottsbluff Experiment Farm, showing the greater vigor of growth from the immature seed. Rows designated by *X* are from immature seed; those designated by *O* are from field-selection seed. Photographed July 15, 1915.

In 1915 the plats were run in duplicate and were one-twentieth of an acre in size. They were on land that had been in potatoes in 1914. The results of the experiment are shown in Table XVIII, together with the results of three previous years.

TABLE XVIII.— *Yields of sugar beets on land plowed at different depths at the Scottsbluff Experiment Farm in 1912, 1913, 1914, and 1915.*

Year and number of plats averaged for each depth of plowing.	Yield per acre (tons) plowed to a depth of—				
	4 inches.	8 inches.	12 inches.	16 inches.	20 inches.
1912, 2 plats	20.5	18.4	19.4	20.1	16.5
1913, 2 plats	21.7	21.2	20.5	21.3	21.6
1914, 3 plats	14.6	14.0	14.8	14.7	14.4
1915, 2 plats	10.5	12.1	11.2	11.7	11.9
4-year average, 9 plats	16.8	16.4	16.4	16.9	16.1

22

These results show very conclusively that at least on the light soil of the experiment farm there is no significant difference in yield resulting from different depths of plowing where the other tillage operations are the same. It is obvious that the deeper plowing is more expensive and on that account is not to be recommended.

METHODS OF CULTIVATION.

In order to determine whether the depth of cultivation had any effect on the yield of sugar beets, a small experiment has been conducted. In this experiment four methods were used in comparison with a check plat. The resulting yields of beets are shown in Table XIX.

TABLE XIX.— *Yields of sugar beets given different methods of cultivation at the Scottsbluff Experiment Farm in 1915.*

Method of cultivation.	Yield per acre.	Method of cultivation.	Yield per acre.
	Tons.		Tons.
Very shallow	9.7	Shallow at first, then gradually deeper	9.6
Deep	9.4	Check, ordinary method	10.5
Deep at first, then gradually more shallow	9.2		

It is apparent from these results that the variation in plat yields is within the range of experimental error and that no difference in yield is indicated as a result of different depths of tillage.

COOPERATIVE DAIRY WORK.

The Nebraska Agricultural Experiment Station, which is cooperating in the support of the Scottsbluff Experiment Farm, has placed seven head of cows on the farm. These cows have been used in the pasturing experiments previously mentioned in this paper, and accurate records have been kept of the milk and butter fat produced and of the feeds other than pasture that have been consumed. In addition to these dairy records, an account has been kept of the feed required and the cost of raising the calves produced by these cows.

It is believed that the information obtained, even from so small a herd, may be important, because of the fact that the combination of feeds which can be utilized in this locality is different from those available in the older dairy sections of the country. Very little is known as to the possibilities of the dairy industry in the Great Plains. The results of this dairy work will be published elsewhere.

Approved;

WM. A. TAYLOR,
Chief of Bureau.

JUNE 10, 1916.